GRASS SONGS

Grass Songs

by Ann Turner

Illustrated by Barry Moser

HARCOURT BRACE JOVANOVICH, PUBLISHERS

San Diego • New York • London

Text copyright © 1993 by Ann Turner
Illustrations copyright © 1993 by Barry Moser

Printed in Singapore

Library of Congress Cataloging-in-Publication Data
Turner, Ann Warren.
Grass songs: poems/by Ann Turner; illustrated by Barry Moser.
p. cm.
Summary: A collection of seventeen poems describing
the experience of traveling West during the 1800s,
as seen through the eyes of pioneer women.
ISBN 0-15-136788-4   ISBN 0-15-636477-8 (pbk.)
1. Women pioneers — West (U.S.) — Juvenile poetry.
2. Frontier and pioneer life — West (U.S.) — Juvenile poetry.
3. Children's poetry, American.   [1. Women
pioneers — West (U.S.) — Poetry.   2. Frontier and
pioneer life — West (U.S.) — Poetry.   3. American poetry.]
I. Moser, Barry, ill.   II. Title.
PS3570.U665G7   1993
811'.54 — dc20   92-11684

First edition
A B C D E   A B C D E (pbk.)

FOR JANE YOLEN,

with love and affection

—A.T. & B.M.

CONTENTS

INTRODUCTION

HOT, drying winds and drenching down-pours. Oxen that get foot rot and go lame. Four children with the "summer complaint" if you are lucky; cholera, if you are not. A river that rises and drowns your cattle and, perhaps, your child. A husband who doesn't know the route and fights with the other men about the best way to go West. Indian tribes. A flat prairie with no tree to hide behind, no place for physical modesty. A body nine months pregnant, struggling up and down mountains. You might reach a settlement in time for the birth; if not, you settle for the wagon in a rocking wind. Could you survive?

Many nineteenth-century women and girls did survive the hardships and dangers of the trip West. They wrote about the journey in letters home and in their private diaries, often using a vivid, homespun style. Their writings are the inspiration for this collection of poems. A few of the poems are based on actual historical figures. Olive Oatman was captured by the Apache and sold to the Mohave Indians. When recaptured by Anglos, she tried again and again to get back to her Indian husband and children.

As a friend wrote of her, "She was a grieving, unsatisfied woman who somehow shook one's belief in civilization. In time we erased the marks from her face but we could not erase the wild life from her heart."*

Another, Arvella Meeker, along with her husband, thought Plains Indians should plow and sow the land. The Meekers' foolish and high-handed ambitions were finished in a deadly raid.

In most families, the men made the decision to go West. Few women wished to leave their friends and family. However, the young women and girls who did love the adventure gloried in the lack of restraint and were happy to be out in the wild air, free at last. And once they arrived, they put down roots, planted orchards, and took on the work of making a new home.

Their courage and resilience in the face of loss, disaster, and constant change inspired me. I wanted to give voice to these women as they journeyed West, as they cared for children under impossible conditions, as they formed communities in the wilderness. We have inherited their homes and their villages, and we are the richer because of it.   — ANN TURNER
June 1992

*Lillian Schlissel, *Women's Diaries of the Westward Journey* (New York: Schocken Books, 1982, p. 69.)

Grass Songs

Glad to Be Gone

I ran through the rain,
the rest huddled in oilcloth
or canvas,
afraid, each one,
of wind and rain.
I love
the needles on my face,
the wind under my dress,
my hair strung out behind.

No one knows the confinement
of woman, sitting,
standing, bustled and trussed,
never allowed to run — sometimes
to dance demure.

I was the only one
who never wept for home.
I scream into the wind,
race after cattle,
pluck the black river fruit,
and reach so high my waist tears,
and no one can say
I am not a lady.

Last night I washed clothes
in the moonlight, the river
soft and dark. I
dove, the water black-
streaming, the light
on my body.
I cried for its newness.

Now I watch
the canvas flap in the wind,
and I, like a sailor,
joyed at the rigging,
the slap and rush of the wind,
the land a wild sea
ahead.

Night's Beads

At first I could not tell my fear;
it had too many names.
But the wind pushed me into the wagon,
into my blue flannel nightgown;
I tied my cap down tight
and under the covers breathed prayers
to all the names of darkness.

Cat, are you there?
Sleep, cat, sleep.
Wolf, do you howl?
Quiet, go another way.
Snake, do you coil?
Swallow your breath.
Mountains, will you break us?
Let us by.
Rivers, do you reach for us?
Sink down, disappear.

Body, are you wounded?
Bleed not.
Child, will you be born?
Rest and wait.
Mother, do you grieve?
Think of me.
Husband, have you forgotten?
Remember.

These are the beads I tell each night.
Sleep will come
at the end of the beads,
and the journey will end
when the names are told.

Raspberry Graves

You remember the April rows,
straight and prickly, all stiff
in their red-bound skins,
and how I knelt with my leather gloves,
eyes shut, wrestling the canes
out — the spent canes down.

That summer you netted the berries,
white that blurred the red underneath,
and I made jam so tart
it puckered our lips,
and you said, "Sweets
for the sweet."

You marked the rows with crosses,
a frame
for the netting.
I laughed and called them
raspberry graves.

Now the road to Sacramento
is dry and dusty.
We lost five in Arthur's wagon
to the bloody flux;
that stream was alkali,
poisoned the cattle —
we left them behind.

We dug the dead in quick,
still afraid of Indians,
with rocks on top
for the wolves;
the sun so hot.
We muttered a prayer
and drove on.

Then Lonnie's wagon
got cholera;
yellow-faced they died
and dropped under the white
wagon top,
the oxen rumbling on
until we stopped
and heard no sound.

That was six; the baby, too,
in a grave so small
it could've been a rabbit's,
and over each grave you built
a wooden cross
already gray.

Everyone's got tales.
Dirt and wind
and drownings come rivers,
flux and fever,
broken axles and oxen gone wild
down the mountain; but I always think
of that trail we left behind,
one grave, two graves, ten,
then twenty,
marked by crosses
like raspberry graves,
only no one
to tend them.

Amanda Hays

I carried it all
the way west under
the wagon seat,
black with one gold stripe,
the letters burned
into the cover.
Sometimes when I was frightened
I reached down and touched
THE ODYSSEY.

John thought my mind
fixed on clothing,
washing, and children one day
to come (oh, not too soon).
He did not know
of reading by moonlight,
dreams of sweet lands,
horses, rocks, green hills,
men with wine in shallow cups,
and women singing high, then
low, arms outstretched to me.

And I would dance naked
under the stars,
name of the god under my
tongue like a wafer,
my hair black as sky;

and the god would come
and take me by the hand,
lead me to the mountainside,
where he would plunge
into me so deep
I cried out his name
sprung from under the tongue.

John doesn't know
I know. He's never touched
me that way. No one has.
But I know it in my body
the way a horse smells water
on the wind.
If I see it, I'll take it.
If I find it, I'll follow it.
And in one sweet leap
I'll leave the shuffled
wagon trail, the dirt and flies
and leathered touch
of untaught hands
for crushed pine
under my back,
my eyes falling
into the stars.

No Time Enough

They want what they want
and they want it now.
No matter Abilene's baby sick
with ague and Mrs. Hartshorn
in labor. "One day is all we'll take,"
they said.

Ever try and have a baby in a day?
Not for a first,
and not for a last; poor
Mrs. Hartshorn, a ropey,
wrung-out woman.
I helped with the rags
but her cries drove me out
and a sick, sweetish smell.

Her face, too, puckered and
white as her lace nightcap
("I *always* has my babies in this!").
I tied it; the chin strings trembled;
she clutched a dried clover
and gasped and moaned and pushed
and the smell rose like fog
but nothing came.

I jumped down and ran
to Calley, smoking by the fire.
"Can't we wait?
She's trying so hard."
He spat; the fire sizzled.
"No, we're late already.
Snow comes in the Blue Mountains,
we're dead. Better one
than all."

All through the night the moon swung
overhead.
A late flower bloomed,
sticky-sweet; something buzzed
and plunged inside, that white cup
nodding and bobbing just
like Mrs. Hartshorn's cap
inside.

Come morning Calley yoked
the oxen, that clanking, dreadful
sound; the splayed hooves shuffled.
Children ran and cried and I, so scared,
put my head in the wagon
to a great stillness.

There Rebecca Hartshorn lay,
a tiny red scrap on her arm
like something the butcher left,
her face seamed and yellow,
tallow melted in the sun.

The women ranged around;
one fanned a fly away;
sister straightened the wilted cap.
Another sighed, "Leastways, she had
her babe in time."
"Yes," they breathed, "in time."

"I'll tell Calley to dig that grave."
I moved back. "You do that!" spat
Rebecca's sister, "and you tell him,
tell him —" her hand punched the air —
"no time's enough for . . .
no time's enough."
She threw the clover out the door.

I stepped down; the baby twitched
like a new-caught hare;
someone did something with a rag;
the wagon seemed smeared
and jumbled
and strangely sweet.

Sweet Pick

They spent all day by the river,
the men up to their waists,
splashing and hollering,
and the kids with us
so as not to see them
in their skins,
as if we cared.

We were after berries and fruit,
a fresh taste for cornbread
and pancakes, our tongues
stuck with the gum of
salt fish, pork,
and beans.

Lonnie found the trees
tucked into a creekbed,
so high, so thick and full with fruit
we reached and shrieked and plucked
and the children ate till
their mouths were black,
and the buckets filled
to the rims.

We came back under a dark sky
with twelve buckets full,
the children asleep on our shoulders,
the men quiet now by the fire.
We sat and ate our bread
with fruit mashed on top,
spilling over the sides,
our tongues plunging into the
sweet black plums.

Out of the Dark

So fast she came
whirling out of the dark,
her dress part of the earth,
dirt on her face, eyes running
with blackness; seems it was tears.

"Safe," she cried, "safe
at last, take me in, I beg
of you!" I sat her
by the fire, bathed her hands
and face, the left hand clawed shut
so stiff I could not open it,
and all the time she told
a story of betrayal,
wagon lost, attacked,
child taken, and she belly-flat
in the pine brush;
"Indians!" she said
and stopped.

I saw how all the women
looked behind in the dark,
dabbed their lips, fixed
their hair; never would they
be so violated, so undone.

And even after that hand opened
once in the sun like a butterfly,
we walked wide
around her
as if she carried an infection
we all might catch.

Olive Oatman

It was the charcoal they couldn't stand.
Sister Maddy tried and tried
to get it out — bleach and scrub
till my skin peeled —
but the marks stayed,
black as the stripes
on a hawk's wing.

Maddy took my mirror away —
each day I saw those marks
took me back,
away from the silk bustled dresses,
the shoes like vises,
the bobs and nods and mouthy words.

Back to his camp by the river.
Smoke blue as morning,
children so quiet
I was afraid at first.
He brought me tied on the back of a horse.
They took my dress,
burned it, and laughed,
put me in deerskin — so soft —
laid me on a bed of pine
with the skins circled 'round,
a smell of earth and sweat and hide.

I choked on the smell,
couldn't get used to the work.
Water from the river in bark buckets,
firewood in a clump on my back,
scraping the dead things he brought me —
blood, skin, and sinew
torn from the hide
like all I'd left behind.

The women hated me at first;
no one talked, just pointed,
even when my belly grew round.
Nothing changed until the night
my son was born. I'd seen
and heard how it was done.
I grabbed the sinew the old woman gave;
I stuffed my mouth with rags
and pressed my back. No sound,
no sound at all,
until his head burst out so black
the women smiled; I shouted, then.

He loved me the way a hawk loves.
I'd seen them once,
talons locked in air,
falling over and under each other,
screaming,
my God, I tried to tell Maddie
she stopped her ears,
I'd forgotten the right words.
You never can go back — once you know.

Three sons in four years.
Learned how to bead moccasins,
dig cattail roots,
weave mats, and split a hare open
in one slit. I was rich as a moon
in the sky, the stars around.
That day by the river
I heard them too late,
smelled them too late,
tried to bury myself in sand;
they caught my hand
and threw me on a horse. "Home,"
they said.

Took my deerskins away,
stuffed me in black silk —
what had I done wrong?
Scrubbed all day at the tattoos.
Kept watch on me day and night,
for years and years.
I could not go back
to the circle of hides,
my three sons like stars,
and Him — no words for that.
I never forgot,
and when I see hawks sailing high,
talons outstretched
in a wild, tumbling fall,
I cry.

Married Now

It was the bluebells
he gave me,
bunched like a September sky
with wisps of green straw
between.
His hat shaded his eyes,
jacket poked out
at the elbows,
but I hardly saw.

Alice was married in town,
in a gown of white,
lilacs in her hair, and three
silly sisters at the rear
like sitting hens;
and her man had a mouth
like an iron hoop.

Lila married on the Missouri,
in a blue dress,
on the ferryboat.
She threw flowers
in the water for luck.
Jake danced her up and down
while Andy played the flute.

My Jeb looked good,
and I stood with him that night
in my green-sprigged dress.
The oxen blew and stamped;
the wagon tops slapped in the wind.
Preacher joined us up,
told us to be good,
and Ma baked a dried-tomato pie,
so sweet a start.

That night, in the wagon bed,
such a fumble — they say
you'll know come time.
I didn't, nor did Jeb.
So glad when I heard
those whoops
and the wagon began to rock.

Out we climbed, into the darkness,
the canvas cover
flapping like a sail
as we jolted over the prairie.

Jeb held my hand.
I liked that.
He took my nightcap off,
and my hair blew out
like a black flag

in the prairie wind,
his rough hands on my face
and the wagon rocking
took me,
and the sounds of the men
and girls laughing
like leaves falling.
Someone banged a pan,
another blew a Jew's harp,
and sudden, I took Jeb's hand
and said, "I'm glad I'm married. You?"

He nodded, gave a shrill whistle,
and stood on the seat
as we rocked to a halt.
They handed up flowers
and a warm loaf of bread.
"Keep your strength up," they joked
and left us.

Outside I saw a star
shoot down the sky, smelled
that sweet grass wind,
and cried — for no good reason.

Make One Woman

There is a better way
to make a woman.
Cut her from cloth, gabardine,
so strong and fine
it will not stretch or tear.
Sew eyes of black
that will not cry.
Paint one nose not over-
particular about cattle
smells and prairie ills.
Fashion two ears
that do not listen
for love,
that are content
with the wind and rain
and sleet.
Stitch her hair down tight
so the blizzard will not
tear it off.
Make those arms strong
enough for horse, harness,
and frozen wood.
Get two legs that will not
ache, that walk a prairie
like a city street.
And feet — do not forget

to make them long and large
for river fords and
winter boots.
Did I forget the heart?
Sew one red outline,
no shading in between.
It will not feel a child
gone, a husband cold,
a home left behind
like a favorite patchwork
quilt.
I would have lasted,
had I been of thread,
cloth, and buttons.

Stones Speak

All day, since first light
we had been traveling.
Not a bird, nothing furred,
just rock and shadow
and a light that made the stones
look bloody.

The oxen's feet were red,
their backs wet and black;
their tiredness made gray clouds.
The only thing moving,
a lizard scuttling fast.
He knew enough to seek cover.

Ned sat, jaw slack,
Chris and Eddie were quiet
in the wagon back.
No wind blew.
I thought I heard the stones speak,
a mute clicking
like crickets buried
beneath the desert sand.

Burning

The leaves drop down
so sudden here;
no one tells you fall comes
like a pony rider posting
hard,
one moment green,
then yellow fire on mountains.

We were not so quick.
Cattle dead, oxen lame,
an axle gone to pieces,
and sickness — no one tells you
days come you cannot sit
to ride.
I lost myself all over
the prairie.

And now, November.
We are just at the mountains.
Snow in the fir, and ice needles
on the ground.
I saw a hawk take wing
and soar over the mountaintop
so sure, so clean
I cried.

We are clumsy with our legs
and arms and needs.
A hawk feeds once each day,
sometimes less,
while we must haul our bodies,
bureaus, churns, and mirrors
up a slope we
cannot pass.

We will build a hut,
butcher the oxen, and burn
all our goods. Come spring,
we'll walk out on foot.
Sam says I am young enough
still.

The ax thumps down,
the oxen smoke in the cold air;
I must run to help;
and if God is good,
once we cross the peak
I'll say we ate our beasts for food,
slept at the foot of a mountain,
and kept warm by a burning bureau.

Arvella Meeker

I wanted to teach them
to plow
a straight, dark furrow,
the earth lifting up
like a mother's hands
to receive her seed;
and over the dry, dusty land
(yielding nothing of benefit),
there would be a soft
green haze.

I wanted them clothed,
that skin so strange a burnish,
to put a screen between the wind
and them, the sun and them,
before that god of theirs
who eyed them naked
on the plain below.

I wanted them to sit in rows,
to hear the Bible's word
and mathematic sums,
the glory of spelling
on a hard, wooden bench,
to feel themselves upheld
and circled round
with learning — to be safe.

I wanted them to marry
with a preacher's words
to purify and bless,
not this quick taking
under a forgetful god,
not this rushing to breed,
a heedless waste of womankind—
I'd seen them die
under their skins.

So much I wanted,
all for the good;
none of it came to be.
The children we sheltered, gone;
the farm we made,
the men we taught, gone
in a fury of anger,
and mine to pay—his body
dragged 'round the farm.
(I hid in the milkhouse
and could not see.)
Some say they drew him like a plow
through the earth,
but I cannot believe that,
even of them.

And what is left
of all my wants and wishes?
A face that slides sideways,
an eye that tics,
a mind that skitters at least noise;
sometimes I think I see myself
drawn through the earth
and wonder
if I might not be more use
that way.

Found

You remember that bitter woman?
The one with the hand clawed shut
who crawled belly-flat in the bushes
after her child
but lost all?

She came west with us,
rolled her piecrust out,
helped with my three
when the fever came.
At times I'd catch her
looking at mine curled in sleep,
and I was afraid.

Nick tried to court her
but she waved him away with that shut hand.
No one came close after that.
Only the children she'd speak to,
soft at night; sometimes she'd
sing about cotton and races
and bets lost.

Then California and the coast,
that swing of blue
made my heart lift up;
even hers, I could tell.
She smiled once at the sun
on the water.

We settled into camp
until news came
from twenty miles away
of a little one taken
from Indians.

She set off on muleback alone;
two weeks gone I got a letter,
the writing small and
crabbed. "Dear Lucy, I found
her well. Thank you for all
you done for me. My hand
is fine. Mary."

She gave her name to us,
and I wished
I could have seen her with
her girl; did she speak
and smile and cry out? Or
did she just slide off her mule
and say, "Welcome back"?

Marnie Goodhue Adams

Every time I climb in
the same.
White nightgown,
ruching scratches my chin,
the nightcap Mother made —
you take it off and spread my hair
black on the pillow
and put your nose to it
like a horse to water.

And your union suit,
white, too; the buttons seem
to hold you in — but not enough.
I love the smell of you
and how my hair beds us
and your hand on my breast, soft
as a butterfly on mallow.
Even your breath is sweet.

And we forget for a time
the daily countings,
the diapers, missed meals,
eating standing in the field,
the clouds like some fierce sentry,
and always the worry.
"Will it be this year or the next?"
Sell, buy, plant, save; wipe
the child.

It's not enough.
The white, the buttons,
sweet smell—
it is death   there
each time you dive
into me
death
each time in your arms encircled,
each time your head flat
on my breast.

In the bed,
four children, soon five;
someday I will not
come back,
someday that head bursting out
will take me with it,
shred by shred,
red spread like hair on the pillow,
and all this for one sweet
breath.

Let There Be

I'd give my soul
for a pot of tea
and a cup with pink flowers,
to sit on a chair with a padded seat,
with a crisp white cloth before me.
Outside the window
(made clean and sparkling with vinegar)
let there be magnolia trees
thick with blossoms;
let there be five cows grazing,
their udders swinging fat and low.
Let there be two children, only—
one in high black buttoned boots,
swung into the sky,
her dress flung back;
and one in a sailor's suit
fresh from the washing.
He is never peevish and tired.
Let there be one dog,
a yellow, friendly hound
who sleeps all day under the tree
with nothing more to do
than nose the wind and bite a fly.

In the distance,
past the thick green lawn,
let there be a river, slow and safe,
with slope-bottomed boats going by
and men singing in bits and catches.
I will sing to them from the porch
and rock in a white wicker chair.
I will stare into the distance
and turn the leaf of a new book.

I will not look for Indians,
a ragged moving on the horizon.
I will not taste the dust
or brush it from my hair one hundred times.
I will not reach for the medicine chest
and pour out castor oil
for Lonnie's severed foot.
I will not remember the oxen
and how we left Big Jake to die by the road.
I will not see Nat and Mannie
rolling in the dust, fighting
over the way to take.

Let me be home on the porch
and I will never ask to see my dead mother's
face again,
I will never ask for happiness,
I will not ask that I grow old;
just give me a porch, a song,
peace.

Cimicifuga

Mother dug it
before I left,
back straining in blue serge
under the Arkansas sun.
She handed it to me quick
like something too hot to hold,
packed in red dirt
raw as the devil's fingernail.
I have carried it all the way
west to Oregon.

It rains each day.
Nat got rheumatism
in the joints,
building the cabin,
and Cilly almost died
twice.
Oxen've got foot rot,
but the horses, Dan and Tucker,
roll in the wet green grass
like seals in the waves.

I dug a garden.
Wrapped Cilly up tight
in my blue shawl,
sent Nat off with bear grease
on his back,
and put my foot to it.
Dirt hardly budged,
dark and thick and wet.
I had to pick it out
with an ax.

I forked in leaves and straw,
took what leavings there was
from the chickens,
and footed it over again.
The snakeroot looked dead,
the taproot dark and tired.
All the little hairs
shriveled on the way.

I looked out last night.
Nat's back kept us awake
and Cilly snuffled
at the foot of the oak bed.
Stood in my nightshirt
on the splintery floor
and thought of Arkansas —
tea on the lawn under the linden,
magnolias white
by the porch,
ladies swishing
up the steps like wind.

I looked again,
under the moonlight.
Two, maybe three leaves
made a small green circle.
Nat sighed and turned over.
Cilly hiccuped and was still.
It will be up soon,
that tall green spire,
and at the top, the blossom
like a flaming candle
to show me the way.

The drawings in this book were executed in graphite
on Crown and Sceptre paper handmade by Simon Green
at the Hale Mill, Maidstone, Great Britain, and are based
on historical photographs of actual persons.

The text type was set in Galliard
by Thompson Type, San Diego, California.
Color separations by Bright Arts, Ltd., Singapore
Printed and bound by Tien Wah Press, Singapore
Production supervision by Warren Wallerstein and David Hough
Calligraphy by Barry Moser
Designed by Barry Moser and Camilla Filancia